Algy's Amazing
Adventures
IN THE
JUNGLE

Algy's Amazing
Adventures
IN THE
JUNGLE

Kaye Umansky

Illustrated by
Richard Watson

Orion
Children's Books

First published in Great Britain in 2013
by Orion Children's Books
a division of the Orion Publishing Group Ltd
Orion House
5 Upper Saint Martin's Lane
London WC2H 9EA
An Hachette UK Company

1 3 5 7 9 10 8 6 4 2

A catalogue record for this book is available
from the British Library.

ISBN 978 1 4440 0685 8

Printed and bound in China

www.orionbooks.co.uk

To Freya and Elinor

Contents

Chapter 1   11

Chapter 2   21

Chapter 3   31

Chapter 4   39

Chapter 5   51

Chapter 6   69

Chapter One

Algy didn't like his new house. Nobody had lived there for a long time. It smelled funny.

He was in the garden. He kept getting in the way of the removal men, so his parents had sent him outside.

Bang!

That was the sofa dropping. Algy jumped. He hated loud noises.

There were lots of things that Algy didn't like. Top of the list was his own name.

Algernon Pugh.

Algernon was just weird. Pugh sounded a bit like – well, never mind.

Here is the list:

My name
The dark
Spiders
Girls
Being kissed by
Aunty Sue
Snakes, crocodiles
and mad tigers
Carrots
Moving house

Algy's parents had told him that moving house would be an adventure. Algy had added that to the list too. *Having Adventures.* No thanks. Too scary.

The garden was a mess. The fences were leaning over, and in a couple of places, missing all together.

Suddenly, a voice behind Algy said, "Hello."

A girl was leaning on the wobbly fence. She had dirty wire glasses, mended with sticky tape.

"Hi," said Algy. He didn't trust girls. They whispered too much. And giggled.

The girl said, "What's your name?"

"Algy."

"What's that short for?"

"Algernon," said Algy. "Algernon Pugh."

"I'm Cheryl-Anne Kristabel Rosalie Smellie. Cherry for short."

Yikes! Cherry Smellie. This girl had an even worse name than he did.

"My mum made it up," she said. "Except for Smellie. We're stuck with that."

There didn't seem much else to say, so Algy said, "'Bye, then," and went to explore the garden.

Chapter Two

At the bottom of the garden was a shed. It had a small, cracked window.

Algy rubbed it, trying to peer inside.

"You can't see," said Cherry from behind. "I've already tried. And the door won't open."

Algy felt annoyed. Who did she think she was, coming into his garden, telling him about his own shed?

He ignored her and gave the door a push. Well, it was his door. He'd decide whether it could be opened or not.

"It's locked," said Cherry.

"I can see that," said Algy.
This time he gave the door a kick.
Crash! The door burst open.
"Hooray!" cheered Cherry.

Together, they stared into
the shed.

Now that it was open, Algy
wasn't sure he liked it.

It was dark in there. There
were cobwebs. Cobwebs meant
spiders.

"Let's go in," said Cherry.

"No point," said Algy, backing away. "Nothing to see."

Well, there wasn't, apart from some rusty garden tools and an old wooden box in a corner.

"Could be treasure." Cherry pointed to the box.

"Who'd leave treasure in an old shed?" said Algy.

But Cherry was already inside, trying to get the lid off.

"Come on," she said. "This is exciting. Give me a hand."

Algy wished she would just go away. She was taking over. But if he didn't help, she'd probably tell her friends he was scared, and they would whisper and giggle.

Watching out for spiders, he stepped towards the box in the corner.

"You pull and I'll push," said Cherry. "Ready? Go!"

Algy pulled. The lid of the box flew back. He fell into the back wall of the shed and a plank fell outwards with a crash…

"Empty," said Cherry. "Never mind."

Algy said nothing. He was staring through the gap where the plank had been …

…into a jungle!

Chapter Three

"Are you okay?" asked Cherry.

Algy still said nothing. This was impossible! How could there be a jungle growing behind his shed?

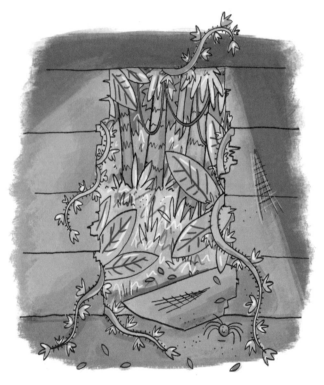

"Oh, wow!" gasped Cherry. "What is *that*?"

"A jungle," said Algy. A butterfly fluttered past. It was *huge*.

"It can't be," said Cherry

"It is, though," said Algy. "I think it must be some sort of – other world."

Algy's tummy gave a flip as he said that. *Other World*. That was definitely going on his list.

"Wow!" said Cherry again. "Amazing!"

Algy could think of a better word. *Scary.*

"Let's go and explore," said Cherry. "It'll be an adventure."

Algy didn't want an adventure. He wanted to run indoors and pretend that this wasn't happening. Jungles were dangerous, everyone knew that.

"I'm not sure," he said.

"Well, I am," said Cherry.
She wriggled though the gap and
stepped out on the other side.

"Hurry up!" she called.
"What are you waiting for?"
Algy hesitated. Could he?
Did he dare?

Well, he wasn't about to let Cherry go on her own. It was his shed after all. He took a deep breath and squeezed through.

Chapter Four

The air in the jungle felt hot and sticky. Something red flashed high in the trees.

"Look," said Cherry. "A path. Let's follow it."

She began moving down a narrow trail.

"Wait!" called Algy. The trouble with Cherry was she never stopped to think about things.

Algy couldn't let her go off on her own. What if she got lost, or eaten? How would he explain it to her mum?

He went after her, glancing nervously back at the shed, in case it vanished. Right now, his new house seemed a lot more appealing.

"I've always wanted an adventure," said Cherry, when he caught her up.

"Hm," said Algy.

"My glasses are steamed up. You go first," said Cherry.

"Oh," said Algy. "Right."

He wasn't sure about being in front. Anything could happen. But if Cherry couldn't see she might lead them over a cliff.

Slowly, they moved along the path. Little scuttling noises came from all around.

Suddenly, something long and green uncoiled and slithered across the path in front of them.

Algy stopped. Cherry bumped into him.

"What?" she squealed. "What?"

"A snake," said Algy. His heart was hammering. "It's all right, it's gone now."

He really hated snakes.

He picked up a stick lying under a tree. Snake protection. Better to be prepared.

They rounded the bend, and
Algy gave a shout.

"Look! Monkeys!"

A group of them were swinging
high in the branches.

Algy didn't mind monkeys.
Anything was better than snakes.
"Where?" said Cherry. She was
wiping her glasses on her sleeve.

Then – disaster! The biggest monkey swung down and snatched the glasses from her hand!

"Hey!" yelled Cherry. But the monkey was already up the tree, proudly showing off its prize to its friends.

"Don't panic," said Algy. That sounded weird, coming from him. It must be the jungle air.

"I can't see. Everything's blurry," said Cherry.

The monkeys were moving away. The thief was wearing the glasses. Algy thought it looked like a wise old man. It was actually quite funny.

It wasn't funny for Cherry though. She looked weird without her glasses. Sort of lost and worried. Algy knew that feeling.

"Don't worry, Cherry," he said. "Follow me."

Chapter Five

With Cherry's hand in his, Algy walked along the path. He swiped at the bushes with his stick in case of snakes and kept a close eye on the monkeys above.

The biggest monkey suddenly took off the glasses and threw them away.

"He's dropped them!" cried Algy. "Wait there!" And he took off into the undergrowth.

The ground became very wet under his feet. A horrible smell met his nose. Moments later, he was staring at a pool of scummy-looking water.

A swamp. A green, stinking swamp.

The glasses had fallen onto a floating log a short way in. Not too far. Just a paddle.

"What's happening?" He heard Cherry from the path.

"I'm getting them!" called Algy.

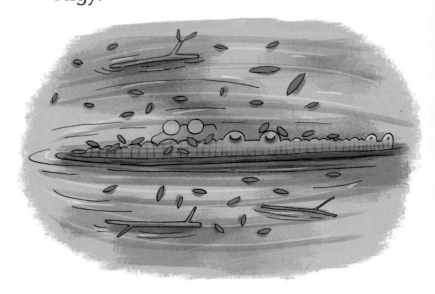

It wouldn't take long. He would do it. Then they could go home.

He pulled off his muddy trainers and socks. Then he pulled up his jeans as far as they would go and waded in.

Water bubbled around his ankles. Mud oozed between his toes. But he carried on, using his stick for balance. The log was just ahead.

He reached forwards and
grabbed the glasses. And then...

...the water churned, and
a huge mouth reared up!

It was red, and lined with rows
of sharp teeth!

Algy lost his balance and fell
backwards.

Splash!

The mouth was moving towards him! This was the end! Help! He was going to die! Unless he acted *right now!*

He brought his stick down with a **whack!**

Back on the path, Cherry was peering around helplessly.

"What's that?" she screamed as a dark shape approached. "Stay away from me!"

"Don't worry, it's only me,"
said Algy. "I've got your glasses.

"Thanks," said Cherry. "I
thought you were a gorilla. What
happened? I heard a splash."

"Bit of a fight with a croc," said Algy. He tried to say it casually.

"A crocodile? *Really?*"

"Or it could have been an alligator. I hit it on the nose, then used my stick to prop its jaws open."

He'd had too. He didn't think he had it in him, but he *had*. He had saved the day.

"Wow!" said Cherry. "That must have been one surprised crocodile!"

Algy wasn't used to impressing girls. He went red. He felt a bit like a hero. It was wonderful.

Just then there came low
growl. Algy turned and saw
something hiding in the shadows.

You couldn't really see it, but
he had the impression of ...
stripes!

There were times to be a hero, and times to run.

"Run!" shouted Algy.

They raced back along the track. From behind, they heard a roar as a tiger leaped out of the bushes.

To Algy's relief, the shed was
still there, just where they had
left it.

"In!" he yelled. "Quick!"

Cherry scrambled through the gap with Algy just after.

He reached back, grabbed the missing plank and fitted it back in place.

Crash!

The shed shook as the tiger hit
the plank head-on.

The plank held.

Cherry and Algy sat panting in the dark. For once, Algy didn't mind. The darkness felt safe.

Chapter Six

That night, Algy lay in bed in his new room. Sleep wouldn't come. He had too much on his mind.

He still couldn't believe it. He had gone into another world. He had rescued a damsel in distress. (Well, Cherry.)

He had seen off a snake
(possibly poisonous), and fought
with a crocodile (or alligator).
He had outrun a tiger!

He had been brave!

He wondered if the jungle would be there the next time he looked. He *would* look, of course. He had arranged to meet Cherry the very next day.

If it was there, would he go back? Maybe. Probably. Cherry would want to.

Cherry was okay, actually.
He would cross *girls* off his list.
And maybe snakes. And *the dark*.
Possibly even *crocodiles*.

Not *tigers*, though. And he still
didn't like carrots, or his aunty's
sloppy kisses.

Would he cross off *having adventures*? Well, yes. Adventures actually weren't that bad.

He'd quite like to have another one.

What are you going to read next?

More adventures with

or go to
sea with

Horrid Henry,

or into space with

Poppy the Pirate Dog,

You could
have fun
on

Cudweed.

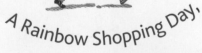

A Rainbow Shopping Day,

or explore

Down in the Jungle,

but watch out for

A Creepy Crawly Story!

Make magic with

The Three Little Witches,

and have
a ball
with

Princesses.

Or follow the star in

The First Christmas.

Enjoy all the Early Readers.

the orion star

Sign up for **the orion star** newsletter
for all the latest children's book news,
plus activity sheets, exclusive competitions,
author interviews, pre-publication extracts
and more.

www.orionbooks.co.uk/newsletters

Follow @the_orionstar on .